Lines From The Heart
♧
Valentine Verses

By Janul

Words of love our hearts combine
I love you; will you be mine?
Poems, feelings meant to be;
Be my date with destiny

Janul Publications

Published by Janul Publications

Copyright © 2009, Jan Knox

Contents

Valentine Verses

Love Is Knowing	6
If	7
Inside My Dream	8
Lonely Shadow	9
Home	10
I Care	11
To Live For You	12
Seclusion	13
Honoured To Know	14
Perfection	15
Direction	16
Today	17
Forever	18
I Miss You	19
Do Not Fear	20
Only You	21
Feelings	22
Coincide	23
Questions & Answers	24

Lines Of Reflection

Message Of Regret	26
The Contest	27
Woman Of Straw	28
An Aggressive World	29
Where Lies The Morning	30
Thoughts	31
Belittled	32
The We That Was Us	33
The Black Empress	34
Date With Destiny	36
Pure Poetry Without Words	37
Regrets	38
The Battle Within	39
Just The Time Of Year	40

I Believe	41
Tomorrow	42
Reflection	43
A Lost Identity	44
Who Am I	45
So Long Ago	46
Many Things	48
The Chain	49
Still I Thought Of You	50

Rhyming Rythms

Just For A Moment I Heard A Song	52
The Writer	54
Girl And Hill & Song	56
The Falklands 1982	58
Smile On The Wind	59
Behind The Crowd	60
Aching hearts	62

Friends For Always

Take Not The Friend	64
The Friend	65
Thoughts For A friend	66
The Message	67
What Is A Friend	68

Christmas

Santa Claus	70
Hello Christmas	71
How Did I Come To Get Me	72
Remember	74

Goodbye

You'll Never Know	76
Goodbye Sweet Dream	77
Goodbye	78

Valentine Verses……..

Love Is Knowing

And love is knowing
That through the loneliness
You are present
Everywhere;
We cannot escape
What has become
Our truth

I too was troubled
That things
Would end
But the blue shade
Passed over

Forgive my darkness
For I cannot express myself
At these times

Be sure in yourself
For my intensity
Matches yours

For always

If

If you can find that person
With whom you harmonise
Who understands your choice
And selects likewise
You will never be afraid
Of rejection

In love
We are confident
Of the answers
To our questions

Therefore
If you can find the courage
To state your desires
You need never be afraid
Of the consequences

Inside My Dream

I am living in a world
Of disenchantment
Through fear of losing you;
You have captured me so fast
And I run into the dawn
Of your arms
Before you can believe
In yourself

I fear myself;
But do not be afraid of me
I believe there is no callousness
In honesty

I cannot be near
Without touch;
Allow yourself
To find me
With your love
Where there are no limitations

Take me
And show me reality

Live inside my dream

Lonely Shadow

Lonely shadow
Hide within
The confines
Of a crowd

But come to me
As a stranger
From behind
That lonely shadow
And shine

Home

When we built
Castles in the air
By throwing flowers
To the wind
We were only dreaming

Perfection is a myth
We could never live with

But contentment
That will become
Our truth

Welcome home

I Care

I care from the heart
Consistently
Deep within my soul

I lie awake too often
Solving your problems
And hoping you will listen

I wonder
Where I fit In
If indeed I belong
In your situation

I am afraid of loneliness
And yet also of love

I cannot hurt you
In my naked truth
But wish to help you forget
Your pain

I can only ask you
Not to hurt me
But in my sincerity
I am always here

I will stand beside you
Where others have deserted

To Live For You

In all needs
You are everything;
I have grown to see you
As all solutions

Though I could
Survive alone
I would not wish it

To care for you is love

To love you is for life

Seclusion

I wanted seclusion
Secluded with you;
Our tiny world
Only one step from fantasy
A kaleidoscope
Of colour
Real enough
To be true

But all I got
Was loneliness
In a world of trivia
Where the time
Was wrong

One day
I shall find
My haven of peace
Where always
We are alone

Together

Honoured To Know

You run rings around me
That shadow
My self assurance
And I find it hard
To compete
In a crowd

But look behind
That transparent veil
Of your easy confidence;
There lies a being
I was glad to remember
And am honoured
To know

Perfection

Today
I believed perfection
To be a myth
Forgetting that
Yesterday
I met my perfection
In you

Tomorrow
I will strive
To see my own world
Bathed
In the glow
Of reflected yesterdays

Perfection

With you

Direction

I want you totally;
But as a cloud of floating rain
I cannot stand still

Silently
I must find the direction
Of the wind

Today

Today
The sun rose
And will set;
It is destiny
The beginning and end
Of this day's fate

Just a day
But a milestone
In your life;
This day
Is special

A day of laughter
And love
As is every day
When I commit myself
Just a little bit more
To you

Forever

I love you
I want you
I need you

Now
I cry for you

Tomorrow
I don't want to mourn
For your love

Things are good

Continue
To love me
For always

As I truly
Love you
Forever

I Miss You

Sometimes
Words are wrong;
Then you are gone

Time must pass
Before things
Are right;
It makes me sad
That you are elsewhere

I am lonely;
I wish to hold you

I am so sorry
That I hurt you

But more so
I am glad
I miss you

Do Not Fear

Perhaps
At last
I reached you
But things
Are on your mind

I want no heartache
And tears

I cannot escape
My dreams;
I express them openly
There is no other way
To reach you

But do not fear
My reaction
To your response

My only wish
Is to know
What you
Desire

Only You

I may appear
To play a dangerous game
With emotions of many

But always
I remain faithful
To the root
Of my infatuation

You

Only you

Feelings

It is necessary
To smile
To talk
Incorporating laughter;
Weary of trivia
And meaningless crowds
I hide my most
Important
Feelings

I miss the presence
Of your wordless soul

I cannot explain
My feelings
Without seeing you

This prolonged absence
Makes me realise
How necessary
You are
In my life

Coincide

Take what you will
And I may give;
Give what you wish
And I might take
Powerfully;
Each of us is whole;
Complete

Never again
Do I wish to join hands
With involvement
Of trivial love
Which destroys the power
Of me
Myself

Now
My only desire
Is to coincide

Questions & Answers

How could I have known?
The only question required
Was why must we ask
Of tears
And smiles?

There are things
Best answered
By the individual solution;
Unspoken realisations
Are often
Better unexplained
And mostly
Unquestioned

Lines Of Reflection......

Message of Regret

I've seen you but a few times
Since the day when I waited
But you never came

Since then, my heart has waited
Patiently
But I can no longer wait
To continue
What should never have been lost
Or forgotten

I never wanted
That summer sensation to end;
Never wanted loneliness
To cast its blackened shadow
Revealing pain deeper than skin

I allowed a new love;
But too soon
One glimpse of you
And it died

Perhaps we were not strong enough
But soon……..

We were
Are
And still could be
Unique

The Contest

Hold me

Whilst you have
My affections

I have come to believe
Though I love you today
Tomorrow
Is always vague

Unintentional;
But there is no guarantee
Or promise

It is merely a contest
Within my heart
For there are so many places
To be seen

Woman Of Straw

You call me
Woman of Straw
Elusive as the fairytale
Of perfection
In a land where we loved

We remember
Fondly
But the magic is gone

Still I need you, my friend,
To cushion my fears
Of disenchantment
Where as one
We tried and failed

As allies
We still have much to offer

Memories

Woman of Straw
Can never return
But wisps of her being
Remain with you

Eternally

An Aggressive World

As we walk
Through our years
Each of us
Wishes for
Eternal peace

Every person
Needs contentment
Within

But ask yourself
If you live
In an aggressive world?

I do

As a result
I am sometimes a very
Aggressive person

Where Lies The Morning

Where lies the morning?
So many times have I woken
To the shadows of first light
But never
Have I witnessed the dawn

Where lies my awakening?
I do not belong in darkness
Yet I would eclipse the sun
Each time the rays
Embrace my soul
For I know not
How to comprehend
The height of my goal

Where lies the answer?
Perhaps there is someone
Who can take me beyond
These complex regions
Of the night

Where lies the morning?
Never would I wish
To take the dawn
And keep it for myself

I crave only to borrow it
To coincide with the sun

Thoughts

These thoughts
Are beginning to hurt

Open your eyes
And read between the lines
Again and again
Until you see
The sincerity
Of my soul
Merge with yours

It's easy
If you try
To forget
A pessimistic past

Belittled

Immersed in uncertainty;
Trapped between the lines
Of seek and find
We are forced to stand;
Emotional magnets
In time and humanity

Each answer
Is a question
Asking more
Of each solution
Until eternity
Would have us content
Within ourselves

It is then
We may find ourselves
Unable to contend
With the result

Belittled
By our own
Perfection

The We That Was Us

The you that was you
Showed the I that was I
How to be
The I that is me

But the you that was you
And the I that was I
Chose separate paths
When the we that was us
Became the I that is I
And the you that is you

Now the I that is I
And the you that is you
Must search
For the them that is they
To become the we that is us
For the we that was us
No longer coincides
With the I that is I
And the you that is you

Anyhow,
May we always retain
That confidence
To be ourselves

The Black Empress

Alone in a crowd
Stood the Black Empress;
Her magic portrayed favourable
Illusion
To those
Who felt her command

Her realm was for those
Never questioning her fantasies
Of perfection
And the insane sanity
Of society

She cast her spell
And won hearts
Listening to their remorse
In quiet release
Of despondency

One day the crowd dispersed;
There was no-one
To hide her aloneness;
No tears left to cry;
No-one cries
For a Black Empress

The curtain remained tight
Hiding her heart
Of softness
Excusing each their faults
Save those of her own

A discreet dreamer
Searching for someone
To cry
In return
For her feelings

Black Empress by image

In truth
The White Witch
Of Love

Date With Destiny

Dream the dreams
Of innocence
And timeless youth
But they slip away
On a wave of regret

Dream the hopes
Of futuristic promises
But progressing years
Will govern you
To know better

Dream the light
Of truthful knowledge
But only pretence
Will keep you
In line with society

Too old to be a child

Dream

But always select
The date with destiny

It is the only way
To know

Pure Poetry Without Words

Shadows of a watery dawn
Unveiled the light for me
On a morning of spiritual discovery;
The sunrise of my thoughts
Revealed sorrow
That I had lived
In perpetual darkness

I was happy to break the bonds;
I took my words into the morning
As we carved our names
Each wishing to be heard

We gained height within ourselves
At the top of our world
Where the sun shone brightly
In the light of day;
At last
We believed
And our words were lost
In meaning

With combined awareness
We felt
Pure poetry

Without words

Regrets

Regrets weigh heavy
In my mind
Regrets
Of what might have been;
Fantasies of emotion
Encased in the love spell
Which could have been mine

But reality
Did not exist;
No chance
To concentrate those ideals
Of perfection

If only reality
Had become
My dream

The Battle Within

Suddenly
I felt as if my love
Had died
Lost
In some outlandish war

They told me
I was not
Alone
There were others
Alike
But I thought only
Of my own situation

Then, they said
We must look towards
Tomorrow
We, who are alike;
The dreamers

But we dwell on memories
To avoid doubts
Which hide
Deep within ourselves

We
The dreamers;
Why, we are
Fighting the battle
Within ourselves

Just The Time Of Year

It's not an easy thing to escape
This state of mind
Although I never pretended
It would be easy;
After all
I've been here before

Suddenly the restlessness grows
And I'm back at the crossroads
Trying to decide
Which road to take

So few are prepared to listen;
But don't say too much
Don't involve them
More than friendly interest allows;
Decisions are yours
And it would be a pity
To lose that friend
The one who cared

Eventually
The darkness will pass

Remember;
It's just
The time of year

I Believe

In the imperfections
Of mankind
Lies living
It keeps us
From uniformity

I believe
In being myself
And each to his own
Never to condemn

I believe in what I am
Knowing myself right
For me

Search no more
I believe
In the future

I believe
In optimism

Tomorrow

Every day
People say
"Work harder"
"Do better"

It can be an asset

It may raise your standards

But to keep up
With ourselves
We must keep trying

Better, better
More………..

Do I work to live?

Or do I live
To work?

My dreams may be here
Tomorrow

But will I?

Reflection

The old man stood
An ache in his heart
Staring at the graveyard

He thought of his friends
Aged, but true
Silently meeting
One by one
Grains in the hourglass

Oh, how they fought
Their weapon was love
As their war claimed its victims;
No bitterness;
The ones who were taken
Granted freedom
To those who were spared

As the years rolled away
And the mist formed
In his eyes
Intensely he prayed;
The horrors of his war
Were never such as those
Today

Progress
In itself
A war
On peace

A Lost Identity

Never thought I'd see the day
When I looked but didn't see
Listened but never heard;
Never thought I'd see the day
When the Freedom Seeker
Gave up

So easy to lie
To the world
Our constant beholder

See myself
In flashes
Of blinding truth

Change is fine
In the right direction

Is it?
Am I?

One day
I will answer
The question

Is this just life?

Or is it
Living?

Who Am I

I am the objective observer
Who only stares at life
So do not lure me
To the rhythm
Of your breathing

So many things
Have passed me by
Yet I see only the things
I cannot touch

My utmost desires
Are merely whims
To the mind of a universe;
So who am I
To place worth
In my sensitivity?

We each cannot question
Our fate

So Long Ago

So long ago
We were strangers
You dreamed innocent adolescence
And I was a baby

So long ago
We were lovers
You saw reality
And I dreamed of growing up

So long ago
We drifted
You saw what had to be
And I stumbled

So long ago
We parted
You released me
And I lost my way

So long ago
We were hardened
You grew indifferent
And I found another

So long ago
We were friends
You felt my confusion
And I cried

So long ago
We confided
You held me in your arms
And stopped my tears

So long ago
We were comforted
You said he was worth each tear
And I saw the envy in your eyes

So long ago
You drove away
You watched me distantly
And I went on dreaming

So long ago
We remembered
You were a beautiful memory
And I thanked you for losing

So long ago

Tonight

Many Things

There are many things
I do not want

I do not want to see you
Pursue a cul-de-sac
Of hopes and dreams
Where you will lose
And take me with you

In contrast
The things I do want
Are infinite

But if only one
Were possible
Catch me walking
On a highway
From the junction
With that cul-de-sac

I will show you
A journey;
A date
With destiny

The Chain

Actions
May speak louder
Than words
But are often
Wrongly perceived
By the self-appointed
Social outcast
Who leaves through fear
Of self revelation
And bittersweet truth

You were needed to maintain
That circle
The candle in the darkness
But you did not believe
Yourself
To be needed

Friend;
I ask no more

But be my soulful friend
Do not be lost

Why did you break
The chain?

Still I Thought Of You

In the cold, heartless dawn
On a day without promise
You were beautiful;
Fate would have us continue awhile
With this kind of love
To borrow each other
In some future moment
Where still I thought of you

We went away
Miles to nowhere
To escape;
But no escape
When still I thought of you

I returned
But you were not there
When I looked out of the window;
Now I fear you forget my name
When I hoped I was winning
When we did not want to lose
The straws we grasped
Within each other

I missed you;
And always
Still I thought of you

And always I will

Rhyming Rythms........

Just For A Moment I Heard A Song

Just for a moment I heard a song
With silent notes; We sang along
With wordless sound; No-one could hear
The understanding born of fear
From separate parts of land and sea
In regions which consumed the free
And tied us to a past affair
To find our comfort if we dare

Who could contend with such a song?
The feeling that we might belong
Again was one from which we ran
For woman can destroy a man
And man in turn may do the same;
The self-appointed victor's game
Where neither sees the other side
And love lies victim, killed by pride

Too bad we cannot know our fate;
The two degrees of love and hate
Are all we know; we've never seen
The answers lying inbetween
Where patience leaves a rose to grow
A perfect bud; So when we show
The actions that could please us all
Our destiny would have us fall

A fleeting glance which caught the eye
Was lost or won? No tears to cry
For in its place will come the day
Us children find a place to play;
Though it be sad if now we lose
Our fate is not our own to choose
Yet not so sad – It was not wrong
If just for a moment I heard that song

The Writer

The Writer sat and gazed, alone
With self made fame he called his own
And with a thought he'd had so long
Created lines of word and song
Describing how he'd ne'er forget
His poet's heart of sheer regret
To see the love he hoped he'd found
Now wounded, bleeding on the ground;
No mortal wound could go so deep
As love now lost; Forever weep
Those sad farewells to passions gone
With nought but dreams to ponder on

The Writer once had dreams to spare
And often sought his comfort there
Until in love, besotted, fell
Into that secret wishing well;
His need to write it ceased to be
He could not dream of poetry
Or write that uncreated song
When love could beckon him along

But all too soon there was an end
To her, his lover and his friend
For one day he recalled a line
'Twas from a piece entitled "Time"
Unfinished…….. And his heart stood still
There was an urge he must fulfil
To reach the end he was compelled
Though loves frail hand would not be held

His pen moved at a furious pace
Now likened to some deadly race
With time.........
         Though when that race was run
He knew not if he'd lost or won

The girl was gone, it had to be
Her patience reached its end, you see
She loved but lost, then tried again
But it would never be the same;
A love once shared was gone somehow
His work seemed more important now
Her lover didn't even know
She took her things and turned to go

The Writer sat so still and sighed
Amongst the many tears he cried
Such self inflicted painful days
But who could love a poets ways?
He put the blame upon himself
For love he'd placed upon the shelf
Experience for him had shown
Why writers mostly lived alone

The old man pondered on the past
A Writer, very near the last
Of many thoughts he'd had so long
Still writing words of verse and song
Describing how he'd ne'er forget
His poets heart of sheer regret
To lose that love he'd known he found
Now dead, not bleeding, on the ground

Girl & Hill & Song

The hill, it rose alone and high
A sceptre raised toward the sky
The ring of trees which crowned its height
Threw shadows; Day became the night
And as the silent night grew deep
The world prepared itself for sleep
To dream the timeless slumber, through
Where fantasy would make things new

A lone girl stood upon the hill
And worshipped darkness black and still
Which housed her dreams & lost her past
But helped her make the present last
The clear still night received her song
With haunting notes so loud and long
And as the moon in brightness shone
All lonely souls were merged as one

"Oh lonely poet, full of fear"
The song went on; "If you were here
I wonder if you'd understand
The omens of our perfect land
Which rise so high above the crowd
Where beauty, pure, can sing out loud
And would your heart become aware
Of Girl, secluded, singing there"

It was the song which named despair
As loss; The wind it stirred the air
And stirred her mind to think of he
The poet whom she longed to see
But could not touch; Stillborn of late
Corrupted by the hand of fate
So did he care? He might belong
One day to Girl, or hill, or song

The Falklands, 1982

Are you crying for me, Argentina?
We've tears of our own still to cry
Yet the hearts of young lovers
All over this land
Would wish you a peaceful Goodbye

Are you crying for me, Argentina?
It's hard to decide who's to blame
But it's never the fault
Of the ones who must die;
Every death causing somebody pain

Are you crying for me, Argentina?
Our young girls will cry when they can
Whosoever did say
It's the good who die young
Was surely a very old man

Smile On The Wind

See a smile on the wind
And borrow it for a moment
Hold it in your heart
And capture the scene
Forgoe the frown
Of a far distant time zone
For life is too lonely
To lose every dream

Behind The Crowd

Once lay my heart so free and true
Where no-one held the mystic charm
Which people thought should have a name
And must belong; They meant no harm
How could they know this spirit free
Have need to live in restless flight
And seek no change in circus crowds
Which help to keep the image bright

But what can lurk beneath the waves
There basking in the murky glow
No lesser beings comprehend?
Their questions mean they cannot know
That far beyond the madding crowd
In regions that be wild and free
I stand removed from all pretence
And witness change from me, to me

I need no burdened words of love;
Await me in some silent land
Where knowledge is the only sign
And promises are grains of sand
Well lost within the mists of time
Where promises are games we play
To feign the scene the crowd would seek
But quiet knowledge paves the way

And in this knowledge may we find
A fire that can leave us free
To be as one, but still be seen
As independent you and me;
We ask no meanings tinged with words
We only build on what is now
And merely wish to coincide
As only we, complete, know how

Aching Hearts

Aching hearts obscure the sun
Playing games which can't be won
Love's reflections oversee
Things we know could never be
How could we have been so blind
Seeking dreams we could not find
Walking, running, learn to fly
Taking risks; the stakes too high

Aching hearts which were so cruel
Feigning love; Expose the fool;
Passion fanned the flames which burned
Hurting others, lessons learned
Childish love through adult eyes
Feelings which I now despise
Things which cannot be undone
Much was lost and nothing won

Aching hearts which proved us wrong
Finding that we can't belong;
You let me down, became unkind;
But my life left you far behind
Where eagles soar, the phoenix rise
Hindsight made me very wise
Oh, how I want the world to know
I'm very glad I let you go

Friends For Always........

Take Not The Friend

Take not the friend
And call him foe;
He who sees darkness
May not command my soul
Whilst I stand in a sunlit meadow
Some call love
Which I name truth

Take not the friend
And call him wrong;
In his time
He was almost love
A token
Of lost chances
An un-detachable scar

Take not the friend
And call him gone;
Reflections
Of our time
Mirrored
In future dreams
Where we will always
Be friends

If only
For the memory

The Friend

Once
You gave me some advice;
The answer was hard
To find

If all friends
Spoke their truth
This world would be a
A palace

Continue speaking your words

Be a friend
To the world

Thoughts For A Friend

Accept me as a friend;
I request no more
For it could not be;
Our ideals are worlds apart

See me as a friend
Who does not try to capture
Your emotions
For the sake of victory

Learn from me as a friend;
Forgive my confidence
My knowledge follows
A straighter path
On which you do not yet walk

Be yourself

Someday in the future
You will not believe
Your thoughts of today;
You, too, will experience
The quiet knowledge
Of yourself

Your indecisions
Will be decisive

And then
You will understand

The Message

Looked in a book today;
Found a card
A belated message

Thanks, friend
But everything
Goes wrong for me;
I need my own solution

Let me die awhile
Quietly

A phoenix
Always lives again;
But this one
Flames and rises
Only
When she chooses

And as a friend
I know
You will still
Be there
When the flames
Reignite

What Is A Friend?

What is a friend?

You won't let me down;
You'll be here
If I have troubles
And listen to my fears;
Dry my tears

You won't lie
To make me feel better;
You'll tell me
Not to overreact
Or when I'm
Out of order
You won't stand
Nonsense

You respect me
For doing the same

We may not meet
For a while;
But when we do
No time has passed;
We are the same

Because
We are friends

Christmas........

Santa Claus

When I was small
I dreamed of Santa Claus
And the magic
Of presents
And turkey

Then I did not believe;
There was no
Santa Claus

Until I met you
And the magic returned

Reality is much nicer
Than a dream

I love you
Santa Claus

Hello Christmas

Hello Christmas
It's good to see you;
Warm house
The smell of food
Happy people
And animals;
Here again
All of us

Many were not
So fortunate

Who cares about
The credit crunch
Or the latest Gucci?

Simple things matter;
Caring
And love

Not much to ask
If you already have it

Think about if you lost it all

Now go
And appreciate
What you have

Today

How Did I Come To Get Me

It's Christmas;
I know this because I'm suddenly
A year older
Being a Sagittarian, you see;
The sights and smells of Christmas
Approached too rapidly
For my empty account
Which paid for
Gaily wrapped presents

But what will I get?
What do I always get?
How did I come to get me for
Christmas?

Not that I stand there glittering
In technicolour wrapping paper
Under the Christmas tree;
Any sparkle
Is merely the early morning dew
Which hung in my hair
As I stumbled and hit my head
On the base of the
Aforementioned tree
Somewhere around dawn

But have you ever noticed
That the first thing
You are aware of
Even on Christmas day
Is yourself?

And so, I awake
Opening the first gift
My eyes
Which focus on
A dull, red glow

I rewrap the package
Carefully
Lowering its container
Gingerly to the floor
Beneath the tree
Of festive glory
Whilst asking myself….

How did I come to get me for
Christmas?

Remember

Remember
When Christmas was young
And wishes were bits of paper
Flying up the chimney
To a far-off
Santa Claus

I remember
When Christmas was young
But now
My imagination
Knows little
Fantasy

Memories
In my own time
And Christmas is old

But still magical

Because
Of you

Goodbye........

You'll Never Know

Why should I feel so down
Over someone I hardly knew?
But I'd like to say Goodbye
Silently
For the sake of the memory

You were the unknown entity
Sent by fate
For my mind to explore
But I never got the chance
To show you
The frail sensitivity
Of my understanding

And so you'll never know
How hard it was
To say Goodbye
Until next time
For I must go back
To where I belong
As is the way of the world

So Goodbye
My friend

Maybe we were best
As a memory
And perhaps it is best
That you'll never know

Goodbye Sweet Dream

Goodbye Sweet Dream
Wild illusion
Though I knew
Your truth

Now I must stray
To some land
Where I cannot love you
As I always loved you
Though always
I will thank you
For those times
When I needed you

Goodbye Sweet Dream
From the dark side
Of the sunrise
Where you are
Scared
To face the dawn

Always I will
Think of you
Fondly;
And the Sweet Dream
In which
We said
Goodbye

Goodbye

Goodbye;
Can I call you
Friend?

Thanks for dropping by
For reading my world
My life
My dreams;
For staying
Until the end
Of the chapter

So much to say
Through the years;
A diary
Of hopes and expectations
Wishes and infatuations
Love

So Goodbye

Or perhaps this is
Hello;
Unlike life
We can turn the pages
Of this book
Back to the beginning
Where we will know each other
Better
At the second reading

www.ingramcontent.com/pod-product-compliance
Lightning Source LLC
Chambersburg PA
CBHW071409040426
42444CB00009B/2164